LOVE

THE
SECRET
TO YOUR

SUCCESS

GLORIA COPELAND

JESUS IS LORD

K E N N E T H
C O P E L A N D
P U B L I C A T I O N S

Unless otherwise noted, all scripture is from the *King James Version* of the Bible.

Scripture quotations marked *The Amplified Bible* are taken from *The Amplified Bible, Old Testament* © 1965, 1987 by The Zondervan Corporation. *The Amplified New Testament* © 1958, 1987 by The Lockman Foundation. Used by permission.

Love—The Secret to Your Success

ISBN 0-88114-798-2   30-0523

10 09 08 07   23 22 21 20 19

© 1986 Eagle Mountain International Church, Incorporated aka Kenneth Copeland Ministries

Kenneth Copeland Publications
Fort Worth, Texas 76192-0001

For more information about Kenneth Copeland Ministries, call 1-800-600-7395 or visit www.kcm.org.

Love—The Secret to Your Success

Love. You hear a lot about it. But, the truth is, few people really know what love is.

For most, it's an emotional phantom that appears—then vanishes—without warning. Illusive. Undefinable. Forever sought but rarely found.

Even believers seem to be confused about it at times. But they don't need to be. The Word of God reveals clearly what love truly is.

Look at 2 John 6. *"And what this love consists in is this, that we live and walk in accordance with and guided by His commandments—His orders, ordinances, precepts, teaching. This is the commandment, as you have heard from the beginning, that you continue to walk in love—guided by it and following it"* (The Amplified Bible).

Quite simply, God says love is keeping His commandments. That brings love out of the indefinite into something explicit. But God has done even more than define love for you. He's given you instructions so that you can know how to love as He loves. By giving you His Word, God has given you His love manual in black and white! All you have to do is follow it, and you'll be walking in love.

If you've made Jesus Christ the Lord of your life, you've already taken the first step of obedience. The love of God has been born within you. But, unless you take action, that love will remain hidden within you. Love works in much the same way as the force of faith. Faith is born into you when you are begotten of God, but until you begin to act on God's Word, that powerful force lies dormant. The same thing is true concerning the love of God. You can have the love of God abiding within you and still be unable to allow this love to work through you and reach other people. Like faith, love becomes active through knowledge of the Word.

That's why the Apostle Paul wrote to the church at Philippi saying, *"And this I pray, that your love may abound yet more and more in knowledge and in all judgment"* (Philippians 1:9).

The love of God is released in your life by acting on the knowledge of God's Word. Without revelation knowledge followed by action, love lies undeveloped and selfishness continues to reign supreme in you—even though you are a new creature.

"But whoso keepeth his word, in him verily is the love of God perfected: hereby know we that we are in him. He that saith he abideth in him ought himself also so to walk, even as he walked" (1 John 2:5-6).

As you act on God's Word, the love of God will be perfected in you. That's when love will begin to flow from you to others.

There is nothing—absolutely nothing—that is more important than learning to love. In fact, how accurately you perfect the love walk will determine how much of the perfect will of God you accomplish. That's because every other spiritual force derives its action from love. For example, the Bible teaches us that faith works by love. And answered prayer is almost an impossibility when a believer steps outside of love and refuses to forgive or is in strife with his brother.

In the beginning of the love chapter, 1 Corinthians 13, the Word says that tongues are just noise if there is no love. If a person has the gift of prophecy, understands all knowledge, and has enough faith to move mountains, without love he is nothing. If he gives all that he has to the poor and even sacrifices his life, without the love of God he gains nothing.

Without love, your giving will not work. Tongues and prophecy will not work. Faith fails and knowledge is unfruitful. All the truths that you have learned from God's Word work by love. They will profit you little unless you live the love of God.

First Corinthians 13:4-8 paints a perfect picture of how love behaves.

Love endures long and is patient and kind; love never is envious nor boils over with jealousy; is not boastful or vainglorious, does not display itself haughtily. It is not conceited—arrogant and inflated with pride; it is not rude (unmannerly), and does not act unbecomingly. Love [God's love in us] does not insist on its own rights or its own way, for it is not self-seeking; it is not touchy or fretful or resentful; it takes no account of the evil done to it—pays no attention to a suffered wrong. It does not rejoice at injustice and unrighteousness, but rejoices when right and truth prevail. Love bears up under anything and everything

that comes, is ever ready to believe the best of every person, its hopes are fadeless under all circumstances and it endures everything [without weakening]. Loves never fails— never fades out or becomes obsolete or comes to an end *(The Amplified Bible).*

That may sound like a tough set of requirements—but you *can* meet them. You are a love creature. God has recreated your spirit in the image of love. And He has sent His love Spirit to live in you and teach you how to love as He loves. You *can* live the love life!

Become love conscious by confessing and acting on God's Word concerning this love. As you meditate these scriptures, see yourself living the love life.

You are the one who has to make the decision to perfect the love of God in your life. No one else can do it for you. So, make the decision in faith and commit yourself to obey God's Word about love.

Let me warn you. There will be times when you would rather do anything than allow love to rule. (It will seem as though it is taking off a pound of flesh!) There will be times when it would be much easier to go ahead and get mad, to seek your own and retaliate.

Love is directly opposed to the senses. The senses have been trained to put themselves and their desires above anything else. They've been trained to selfishly seek their own way. But love, the Word says, does not seek its own rights or its own way. And to walk in love, you must demand that your senses (flesh) be subject to the Word.

Without a definite decision, you will not continue in the love of God. So commit yourself to agape—God's love—now. And when temptation comes, you will remember this decision and obey love.

Once you've made the decision, the most powerful thing that you can do in perfecting the love walk is to continually confess that you are the love of God. Base your confession on 1 Corinthians 13:4-8. This God kind of love will begin to influence all that you say and do. If someone says something unkind to you, love will say, "That is okay. I am not touchy, fretful or resentful. I take no account of that." And you go free!

Learn to believe in love. It is the most powerful force in the universe. Walk in love by faith in the Word. Walking in love is walking in the Spirit. It is walking as Jesus walked.

Love never fails. Nothing works without it, and there can be no failure with it. When you live by love, you cannot fail.

It takes faith to believe that love's way will not fail. The natural mind cannot understand that because the natural man and his world are ruled by selfishness. He believes if you don't look out for number one (himself), nobody else will. And, in a sense, he is right. Nobody else can look out for him. His selfishness shuts the door to the love of God, and he winds up on his own.

But when you practice love by faith and refuse to seek your own, you put the Father into action on your behalf. He will allow no man to do you wrong (1 Chronicles 16:22). As long as you stay in love, God the Father seeks your own. He sees to it that love never fails. Walking in love is to your great advantage!

Agape love is a new kind of power. It makes you the master of every situation. As long as you walk in love, you cannot be hurt and you cannot fail. No weapon that is formed against you will prosper. No one even has the power to hurt your feelings, because you are not ruled by feelings but by God's love. You are loving as He loves.

E. W. Kenyon accurately tagged this agape love "a new kind of selfishness." You no longer seek your own success, yet your success is guaranteed!

This love is revolutionary. If we fully understood the great return from living God's love, we'd probably be competing with each other, each of us trying to love the other more. And without a doubt, everyone would emerge from that competition a winner! For love is truly the only sure secret to our success.

Prayer for Salvation and Baptism in the Holy Spirit

Heavenly Father, I come to You in the Name of Jesus. Your Word says, "Whosoever shall call on the name of the Lord shall be saved" (Acts 2:21). I am calling on You. I pray and ask Jesus to come into my heart and be Lord over my life according to Romans 10:9-10: "If thou shalt confess with thy mouth the Lord Jesus, and shalt believe in thine heart that God hath raised him from the dead, thou shalt be saved. For with the heart man believeth unto righteousness; and with the mouth confession is made unto salvation." I do that now. I confess that Jesus is Lord, and I believe in my heart that God raised Him from the dead.

I am now reborn! I am a Christian—a child of Almighty God! I am saved! You also said in Your Word, "If ye then, being evil, know how to give good gifts unto your children: HOW MUCH MORE shall your heavenly Father give the

Holy Spirit to them that ask him?"
(Luke 11:13). I'm also asking You to fill
me with the Holy Spirit. Holy Spirit, rise
up within me as I praise God. I fully
expect to speak with other tongues as
You give me the utterance (Acts 2:4). In
Jesus' Name. Amen!

Begin to praise God for filling you with the Holy Spirit. Speak those words and syllables you receive—not in your own language, but the language given to you by the Holy Spirit. You have to use your own voice. God will not force you to speak. Don't be concerned with how it sounds. It is a heavenly language!

Continue with the blessing God has given you and pray in the spirit every day.

You are a born-again, Spirit-filled believer. You'll never be the same!

Find a good church that boldly preaches God's Word and obeys it. Become a part of a church family who will love and care for you as you love and care for them.

We need to be connected to each other. It increases our strength in God. It's God's plan for us.

Make it a habit to watch the *Believer's Voice of Victory* television broadcast and become a doer of the Word, who is blessed in his doing (James 1:22-25).

About the Author

Gloria Copeland is a noted author and minister of the gospel whose teaching ministry is known throughout the world. Believers worldwide know her through Believers' Conventions, Victory Campaigns, magazine articles, teaching audios and videos, and the daily and Sunday *Believer's Voice of Victory* television broadcast, which she hosts with her husband, Kenneth Copeland. She is known for "Healing School," which she began teaching and hosting in 1979 at KCM meetings. Gloria delivers the Word of God and the keys to victorious Christian living to millions of people every year.

Gloria has written many books, including *God's Will for You, Walk With God, God's Will Is Prosperity, Hidden Treasures, Living Contact* and *Are You Listening?* She has also co-authored several books with her husband, including

Family Promises, Healing Promises and the best-selling daily devotionals, *From Faith to Faith* and *Pursuit of His Presence*.

She holds an honorary doctorate from Oral Roberts University. In 1994, Gloria was voted Christian Woman of the Year, an honor conferred on women whose example demonstrates outstanding Christian leadership. Gloria is also the co-founder and vice-president of Kenneth Copeland Ministries in Fort Worth, Texas.

Learn more about
Kenneth Copeland Ministries
by visiting our Web site at
www.kcm.org

Materials to Help You Receive Your Healing

by Gloria Copeland

Books

* And Jesus Healed Them All

  God's Prescription for Divine Health

* Harvest of Health

  Words That Heal (gift book with CD enclosed)

Audio Resources

God Is a Good God

God Wants You Well

Healing School

Video Resources

Healing School: God Wants You Well

Know Him as Healer

Books Available From
Kenneth Copeland Ministries

by Kenneth Copeland

* A Ceremony of Marriage
  A Matter of Choice
  Covenant of Blood
  Faith and Patience—The Power Twins
* Freedom From Fear
  Giving and Receiving
  Honor—Walking in Honesty, Truth and Integrity
  How to Conquer Strife
  How to Discipline Your Flesh
  How to Receive Communion
  In Love There Is No Fear
  Know Your Enemy
  Living at the End of Time—A Time of
      Supernatural Increase
  Love Never Fails
  Managing God's Mutual Funds—Yours and His
  Mercy—The Divine Rescue of the Human Race
* Now Are We in Christ Jesus
  One Nation Under God (gift book with CD enclosed)
* Our Covenant With God
  Partnership, Sharing the Vision—Sharing the Grace
* Prayer—Your Foundation for Success
* Prosperity: The Choice Is Yours
  Rumors of War
* Sensitivity of Heart
* Six Steps to Excellence in Ministry
* Sorrow Not! Winning Over Grief and Sorrow
* The Decision Is Yours

*Available in Spanish

* The Force of Faith
* The Force of Righteousness
  The Image of God in You
* The Laws of Prosperity
* The Mercy of God (available in Spanish only)
  The Outpouring of the Spirit—
      The Result of Prayer
* The Power of the Tongue
  The Power to Be Forever Free
* The Winning Attitude
  Turn Your Hurts Into Harvests
  Walking in the Realm of the Miraculous
* Welcome to the Family
* You Are Healed!
  Your Right-Standing With God

by Gloria Copeland

* And Jesus Healed Them All
  Are You Listening?
  Are You Ready?
  Be a Vessel of Honor
  Build Your Financial Foundation
  Fight On!
  Go With the Flow
  God's Prescription for Divine Health
  God's Success Formula
  God's Will for You
  God's Will for Your Healing
  God's Will Is Prosperity
* God's Will Is the Holy Spirit
* Harvest of Health
  Hidden Treasures
  Living Contact
  Living in Heaven's Blessings Now
  Looking for a Receiver

                         *Available in Spanish

One Word From God Can Change Your Life

One Word From God Series:
- One Word From God Can Change Your Destiny
- One Word From God Can Change Your Family
- One Word From God Can Change Your Finances
- One Word From God Can Change
     Your Formula for Success
- One Word From God Can Change Your Health
- One Word From God Can Change Your Nation
- One Word From God Can Change Your Prayer Life
- One Word From God Can Change Your Relationships

Load Up—A Youth Devotional
Over the Edge—A Youth Devotional
Pursuit of His Presence—A Daily Devotional
Pursuit of His Presence—A Perpetual Calendar

Other Books Published by KCP

The First 30 Years—A Journey of Faith
     The story of the lives of Kenneth and Gloria Copeland
Real People. Real Needs. Real Victories.
     A book of testimonies to encourage your faith
John G. Lake—His Life, His Sermons,
     His Boldness of Faith
The Holiest of All by Andrew Murray
The New Testament in Modern Speech
     by Richard Francis Weymouth
The Rabbi From Burbank by Rabbi Isidor Zwirn
     and Bob Owen
Unchained by Mac Gober

Products Designed for Today's Children and Youth

And Jesus Healed Them All (confession book and CD gift package)
Baby Praise Board Book
Baby Praise Christmas Board Book
Noah's Ark Coloring Book
The Best of *Shout!* Adventure Comics
The *Shout!* Giant Flip Coloring Book
The *Shout!* Joke Book
The *Shout!* Super-Activity Book
Wichita Slim's Campfire Stories

*Commander Kellie and the Superkids*_{SM} Books:

The SWORD Adventure Book
*Commander Kellie and the Superkids*_{SM}
    Solve-It-Yourself Mysteries
*Commander Kellie and the Superkids*_{SM}
    Adventure Series: Middle Grade Novels
    by Christopher P.N. Maselli:

#1 The Mysterious Presence
#2 The Quest for the Second Half
#3 Escape From Jungle Island
#4 In Pursuit of the Enemy
#5 Caged Rivalry
#6 Mystery of the Missing Junk
#7 Out of Breath
#8 The Year Mashela Stole Christmas

World Offices of
Kenneth Copeland Ministries

For more information about KCM and a free
catalog, please write the office nearest you:

Kenneth Copeland Ministries
Fort Worth, Texas 76192-0001

Kenneth Copeland
Locked Bag 2600
Mansfield Delivery Centre
QUEENSLAND 4122
AUSTRALIA

Kenneth Copeland
Private Bag X 909
FONTAINEBLEAU
2032
REPUBLIC OF
SOUTH AFRICA

Kenneth Copeland Ministries
Post Office Box 84
L'VIV 79000
UKRAINE

Kenneth Copeland
Post Office Box 15
BATH
BA1 3XN
U.K.

Kenneth Copeland
Post Office Box 378
Surrey, B.C.
V3T 5B6
CANADA

We're Here for You!

Believer's Voice of Victory Television Broadcast

Join Kenneth and Gloria Copeland and the *Believer's Voice of Victory* broadcasts Monday through Friday and on Sunday each week, and learn how faith in God's Word can take your life from ordinary to extraordinary. This teaching from God's Word is designed to get you where you want to be—*on top!*

You can catch the *Believer's Voice of Victory* broadcast on your local, cable or satellite channels.

Check your local listings for times and stations in your area.

Believer's Voice of Victory Magazine

Enjoy inspired teaching and encouragement from Kenneth and Gloria Copeland and guest ministers each month in the *Believer's Voice of Victory* magazine. Also included are real-life testimonies of God's miraculous power and divine intervention in the lives of people just like you!

It's more than just a magazine—it's a ministry.

To receive a FREE subscription to *Believer's Voice of Victory,* write to:

Kenneth Copeland Ministries
Fort Worth, Texas 76192-0001
Or call:
1-800-600-7395
(7 a.m.-5 p.m. CT)
Or visit our Web site at:
www.kcm.org

If you are writing from outside the U.S., please contact the KCM office nearest you. Addresses for all Kenneth Copeland Ministries offices are listed on the previous pages.